First published in Great Britain as a softback original in 2015

© David Sloly 2015

The moral right of this author has been asserted.

UK Book Publishing is a trading name of Consilience Media
www.ukbookpublishing.com

ISBN: 978-1-910223-31-4

Why You Need A Business Story And How To Create It
also available as an ebook.

Why You Need A Business Story
And
How To Create It

For Hunter

Thank You

Nadia Abdulla, Lucy Dawson, Andrew Plant, Chris Roberts, Ian Sanders, Annette Sloly, Harvey Steed, Julie Steed and Emily Warwick.

Contents

Acknowledgments

To the amazing talent working in broadcasting, journalism,
advertising and marketing who over the years have shared with
me practical techniques for finding and shaping stories.

To the big thinkers of the world who through the application
of imagination have created extraordinary stories that have both
educated and entertained me.

Why Choose This Book

This book is thin and I make no excuse for that.

A chap who advises airports on passenger terminal layout once told me that airlines would prefer it if passengers simply slid down a greasy pole straight into their seat ready for take off. On the other hand, the airport operator prefers passengers to slowly zigzag through an endless parade of shops and restaurants, spending as much money as possible. I believe people seeking to improve a skill prefer to get to the point of understanding as quickly as possible.

During the writing of this book I edited out the zigzagging so you can slide down the pole – straight to the insights for becoming a storyteller today. So yes, this book is thin because it's the antidote to all that unnecessary complexity that you will find in other books. Instead of character development, subplot and beats (all important stuff if you are planning to write a Hollywood blockbuster), this book offers a 5-step actionable process that will enable you to create your authentic business stories today.

To help you create your first story I have provided some pointers highlighting different types of business story you can create. Once you have chosen a story theme you will be ready to produce your first business story using my 5-step process. First you will learn how to find the raw facts of your story. Then you will discover what people crave to hear about and how to include it in your story. Next you will learn a well-established formula for creating story structure. Emotional roller coasters will keep the listener engaged and I'm going to show you how to create them; and finally I will share with you a formula for producing killer headlines so that your story gets noticed.

So read on and find out why stories are good for business, where you can use them and the 5-step process that will help you to quickly create them.

CHAPTER 1

The Author's Story

FIRST, LET ME tell you the story of how I ended up here. It's the winter of 1989; having sold my small business I am sitting in my parents' living room thinking that my life is seriously lacking direction. Realising I need something to keep me occupied, I tell my parents I intend to go travelling, expecting them to preach to me on the dangers of the modern world. Instead, my intention is met with a smile. Two weeks later I climbed into my little red camper van and waved goodbye to London, with ambitions of being a European hippy, spending my days picking oranges in the sun and my evenings listening to Pink Floyd.

I spent my first night in France parked next to a remote farm and awoke to a crisp, clear, blue sky and an empty road ahead of me – the perfect metaphor for my new adventure. After getting to grips with driving on the 'wrong' side of the road, I headed to Belgium, Holland and Germany, taking the less clogged A-roads. I was free as a bird and cold as hell. With each new country came a rapid drop in temperature, the final straw coming as I rolled through the checkpoint of the former Yugoslavia, in late November.

There are two pieces of information worth noting about the former Yugoslavia in November 1989: the first is the temperature, which can easily drop to minus ten at night; the second is hyperinflation, driven by rampant bank note printing, that was spiralling out of control at a monthly inflation rate of 313,000,000%.*

To help provide some perspective: my soup would freeze solid within a couple of hours; and as far as hyperinflation goes, per sheet it was cheaper to use low denomination banknotes as toilet paper then actually buy the stuff. The two unusual factors of extreme cold and hyperinflation balanced each other out, as the inflation meant that my British pounds could buy dark rum for the equivalent of just 20p a bottle and drinking it in copious amounts kept the cold at bay.

*http://www.businessinsider.com/10-hyperinflation-stories-of-the-20th-century-2011-3?op=1

In a desperate attempt to get warm and sober, I pointed my van south and headed for orange picking country, Greece. But by the time I arrived the picking had long been done and my rum reserves were all but dry. So one cold morning I decided that I would take a ship from Athens to Israel, where I knew the temperature would be more favourable. I purchased a ticket from a roadside booth just half a mile from the port and then promptly became completely lost trying to locate the ship. At one point, I was sure I could see its funnel in the distance, but it just seemed impossible to get anywhere near it. Desperately lost, I stopped at the side of the road ready to give up and turned the radio on for distraction. Staring out of the windscreen at a chaotic city, I soon found myself completely absorbed by a story on the radio.

The presenter told of a hero setting off on a quest, who was soon battling gallantly against the odds, having to overcome all kinds of challenges, each one adding more tension, until finally victory and reward. But here's the kicker: the presenter told the story in Greek and I can't speak a word of Greek! I had listened to an entire story having not understood a single word yet I seemed to understand everything that was taking place.

I had witnessed the classic three-act story: Act 1 – Problem; Act 2 – Struggle; and Act 3 – Resolution. The three-act story is so widely used that I was easily able to imagine in my mind my own version of the story being told on the radio. It's obvious in retrospect, but at the time I can clearly remember it being a revelation. Stories operate in a universal framework where the characters, places and objectives change, but the format remains roughly the same. So although the story was told in Greek, it was easy for my imagination to superimpose my own version of a story on top of the familiar framework. I made a promise to myself right there at the side of the road that on my return to the UK I would learn to find and tell stories.

Back home I approached the BBC and asked if they would train me to be a journalist. Much to my surprise I got a yes so I spent the next two years learning how to gather information and distil it down to a clear, easy-to-comprehend story. I went on to work in broadcasting, where I continued to learn the art of story, and then I switched careers to advertising where I had the privilege of helping world-class brands find and tell their stories. Now I use the process described in this book to help organisations find and tell their stories.

I hope you enjoy learning how to create your own business stories, using a method that first came to light for me whilst I was searching for some sunshine. Did I catch that ship? Yes, I did, but I wished I hadn't as it sailed straight into a force nine gale. But that's another story.

CHAPTER 2

Why You Need To Find And Tell Your Business Story

THE WORLD IS so saturated with far-fetched advertising promises that they tend to be met with a whiff of general disbelief. Your business needs a new authentic way to communicate why people should engage with you, one that transcends boastful claims. That's where your business story comes in. Nearly every business has a competitor that offers similar – or even the same – benefits, so how will a customer choose which business to buy from? Testimonials? Promotions? Benefits? Your competitor can find half a dozen customers happy to supply testimonials; equally they can run a promotion and they probably share the same or similar benefits. But now tell a prospect 'why' your business exists, a story about how you helped a customer solve a problem and how that has informed the way you design your product and your competitor can't match you. They can try to copy you, but they can't have the same story as you. Your story makes you unique and memorable whether it's about you, what you sell or an emotional vehicle that connects your brand with your audience.

Stories have the advantage that they connect with the audience at an emotional level and when someone or something arouses emotions the part of our brain responsible for memory kicks in. That's why millions of Britons can fondly recall the John Lewis Christmas 2014 TV adverts yet struggle to remember any of their competitor ads. Every year John Lewis delivers a simple yet compelling story and as soon as it airs the social channels light up as people discuss, share and make an emotional connection with John Lewis, albeit via the story of a little boy and his pet penguin (more on the power of cute creatures later). I am sure that at the time the advert was broadcast John Lewis had some splendid offers available. Would the social networks, coffee shops, hairdressers and offices up and down the country be filled with conversation about the marginally discounted price of a washer/dryer? The story, on the other hand, stirs our emotions.

Stories aren't just for the Christmas one hit wonders either. Dove moved the 'beauty' goalposts after Stacie Bright, the Unilever Global Director for Marketing Communications, made a call for real beauty. Stacie noticed that mainstream models in advertising were affecting her daughter's self-esteem, and by default everybody's daughters' self-esteem, so she decided to take action. She created a mock advert using the daughters of Unilever directors and placed messages next to each child proclaiming that these girls believed they weren't beautiful. The mock-up stirred emotions in everyone that watched it and the board signed off the campaign for real beauty without hesitation. Dove went on to double its profits from £1bn to £2bn.

Now I want to share with you another example of a company using the power of story to generate sales. These guys are not household brands like John Lewis or Dove. They have no need for creating Christmas shopping frenzies or to change the way women are portrayed in advertising.

Maersk Line Limited is a global transport company whose ships are certainly not glamorous gin palaces; they are big slow vessels that move containers full of stuff around the world. When Maersk started using stories to show the value they add to the supply chain they witnessed an unprecedented uplift in new business leads. One story the Maersk marketing team told focused on a ship navigating the extreme conditions of the frozen Baltic Sea. When the Baltic freezes ships find it difficult to reach the port and when they can't dock the supply chain gets broken. Yet Maersk has a reputation for successfully navigating those extreme conditions and through storytelling they could show just how much logistical effort it takes to make it happen. Maersk used photos from the trip to help dramatise the story that revealed how the Maersk ship, against the odds, managed to reach the port in ridiculously hostile conditions. The results achieved from sharing the story via social channels? An outstanding 150 leads.

Your stories are totally unique and they enable you to take the fight away from the comparison of rational benefits and into an engaging emotional space, where the real customer decisions are made.

You may not have a burning desire to change the masses' perception of beauty, but you may need to convince stakeholders to go along with a new strategic plan, talent to join your company or investors to buy your stock. The rational facts may provide the evidence and insight but by including those facts as part of a story you can make them easier to digest.

Unless you're an analyst you probably won't get that excited at the prospect of attending a presentation filled with numbers. That said, the general stance for business communication is to make a case using as many statistics as possible. Does this kind of effort actually change behaviour? It's more likely that the people you are trying to persuade are already in possession of their own stats derived from personal experiences. So whilst you are trying to persuade them with your facts, stats, and logical rational arguments, they are busy winning the argument in their heads supported by their preconceptions that are heavily reinforced with their own facts and stats drawn from experience. When people are confronted with crushing factual arguments or information overload they tend to quickly take a defensive stance. You may succeed in presenting a bulletproof intellectual argument, but people are simply not inspired to act by reason alone. They listen but remain sceptical. As Dale Carnegie wrote in his book How to Win Friends and Influence People: "A man convinced against his will is of the same opinion still." But when you share information as a story the defensive guard is dropped. Why? Because when we listen to a story we are not using the critical rational part of the brain; instead we are engaging the older, more emotional part, the same part that hugely influences our decision-making.

It's been well documented by the scientific community that information delivered as a story is far more persuasive and memorable than its purely rational counterpart. Psychology studies repeatedly show how story deeply influences our attitudes, beliefs and decisions. Yet despite the importance that persuasion plays in ensuring you get the outcome you need for your business, most executives admit that they struggle to communicate clearly and fail to inspire.

Research carried out by the Carnegie Institute of Technology reveals that a staggering 85% of individuals' financial success is down to that person's ability to communicate, negotiate, and lead. Just 15% was attributed to technical knowledge. Yet the strange thing is that even the smartest leaders quickly slip into the cold world of acronyms and jargon in an attempt to persuade people to follow them. You know the drill: they open a 60 slide presentation and bulldoze their way through the deck that's stacked with logic.

But as research has shown pure reasoning may make the logical point, but it seldom moves people to action. On the other hand, a well-told story has the ability to communicate directly to the cognitive subconscious and create an emotional reaction, which is important as most changes in attitude and decision-making are made at an emotional level rather than at the rational level.

Not convinced? Take a moment and think back to three of possibly the most significant decisions you have or will make in your lifetime: the career you chose; the home you live in; and the partner you live in it with.

So go ahead and ask yourself: when you last changed job did you honestly seek to weigh up all the possible career choices that matched your personal life goals? Considering the amount of time spent working over a lifetime surely you would have spent weeks analysing your options based on a set criteria? After all, that would be the rational thing to do.

How about your home? Did you honestly list all rational arguments for your current property against all competitive properties and then make your offer based only on the facts? Or did you walk through the front door with the estate agent and say to yourself: "Wow; this place feels perfect!"?

What about your choice of partner, the person you selected to spend the rest of your life with? Did you find yourself falling rationally in love with your partner after extensive research into all other relationship options based on a pre-determined criteria? Or did you find yourself falling in love when you least expected it?

Of course we are experts at post-rationalising our decisions and providing a perfectly sane narrative to justify why we made the life choices we did, but the truth is the real decisions we make, big and small, are made in the limbic part of the brain, the part that handles emotion. We only rationalise those decisions after the event – and let's be honest, if all our decisions were made through the absolute application of rational thinking then we would never actually make a decision as we couldn't physically amass and compute all the possible variables. Without emotion, we are biologically incapable of making decisions.

So what about the serious world of business decision-making? Surely the spreadsheet-driven world of profit and loss has no place for emotion? Well, take a look around your office. Is it filled only with rational business tools? Or does every desk have sleek silver Apple Macs sitting on them running software that would happily operate on a much cheaper machine? What about your company car? Did you elect to drive the Skoda 1.4 diesel with solid paint? Or opt for the Audi? One of my clients signs his documents with a £300 pen! Is that rational? I can buy one hundred perfectly functional pens from my local supermarket for the same price.

If you think that emotions are probably only effective for B2C and won't work for B2B where product specs and value propositions rule the buyer's decision-making then you need to think again. Research carried out recently by Google revealed that B2B brands provoke an emotional connection with more than 50% of their customers. That's compared to 10-40% for B2C. Yep, the emotional connection between buyer and seller for the B2B sale is crucial.

Let's be clear, the real decisions we make in life and in business are hugely influenced by our emotions. Rational facts delivered in isolation are often considered dull, easily forgotten and at worst can be viewed as a threat. But if you take the facts and envelop them with stories they can be transformed into something that provides context, sustains attention and makes them more persuasive.

So if emotions create behaviour change and stories create emotions, why aren't we using more stories in business? Could it be because stories can appear too simplistic in today's complex world? Is it that some organisations encourage staff to communicate via artificial languages and acronyms that don't lend well to storytelling? Or is it the word story? Does that word conjure up negative associations with rumours, tales and, worse still, lies?

I believe the simple reason businesses don't use more stories is that most people have little or no idea how to actually create one. Most of the information available on how to write a business story is either far too complex to be of any use or oversimplified to the point that it only offers a few hints on the subject. That's why I have made it my mission to put down on paper a process that will enable you to create your business story. Don't get me wrong; I am not suggesting that my process is the only way a story can be created – that would be silly. What I am saying is that this process has been tested and proven to work.

To make it as simple as possible, I've broken the process down into five linear steps that are easy to follow. This 5-step process will enable you to quickly create compelling stories that can be used in all areas of your business. Once you understand the process for creating a story, you can tell that story everywhere, regardless of whether you are speaking to one person or blogging to millions.

So if you want to be more persuasive, make the intangible tangible, simplify the complex and connect with people emotionally then it's time for you to understand the basic principles of how a story is constructed.

CHAPTER 3

Ideas For Your First Business Story

BEFORE WE GO headlong into applying the 5-step process for creating your business story, I want to share with you some ideas for stories to tell. The 5-step process will then naturally lend itself to helping you create and shape that story. It works for all kinds of story so it really doesn't matter if yours is uplifting, sad or even humorous as the structure is the same. So if you already have an idea for the subject for your business story, then great, just jump to the next chapter. If you're not sure what story to tell first then here's seven story ideas for you to choose one from. You'll find all of them valuable at some stage, but for now just pick one that works for you:

1) Your Purpose Story

So many companies talk about what they do and how they do it but miss out WHY they do it. Capturing the business's 'why' is often where a compelling story can be found. Use your 'Why' story for new business meetings, to explain the purpose of your company to new staff and to remind everyone why you are in the business you are in.

2) Your Risk Story

Business leaders take risks and every risk has its story, be it success or failure. Either way, these stories tell us about the kind of leader who is at the helm so choose this story if you want to demonstrate how you operate under pressure and how you manage risk.

3) Your Vision Story

Giving people a window through which to view how your company will look in the future will go a long way to helping them understand your strategy and what part they will play in realising your goals. A vision story is the perfect way to make your thinking tangible.

4) Your Customer Story

Get your customers to do the heavy lifting by sharing their stories of where they see the value you add. When we hear these told from the customer's point of view they become more authentic and therefore people are more willing to share them.

5) Your Launch Story

Whether your business is an e-tailer, a tech start-up or a global enterprise you had a launch: a deadline, a day when you went live. Share the story of your journey from humble beginnings and bring to life what you are capable of.

6) Your Founder Story

So many businesses fail to mention the founders, even when they are still running the business. You may be humble, but people want to hear the story of how and why you started the business, the hurdles you faced and what you learned on the journey.

7) Your Leadership Story

Your leadership story can help you guide an organisation. So at your next boardroom meeting you can use the power of story to demonstrate how your leadership skills have avoided potential storms, created new opportunities and put the organisation in better stead.

So let's get started. You have chosen your idea from the list or you have an idea of your own and you are ready to bring it to life. The first step you are going to take is to establish the facts of the story by using a very simple technique called the 5Ws: the who, what, when, where and why. These facts are the raw ingredients of your story. Once you have the facts you will learn how to spot and amplify the juice in those facts and conjure up the very stuff people crave to hear about. Then you will organise your facts using a tried and tested framework and next you will tweak the story flow to bring out the emotion. Finally, you will learn how to create a killer headline so that your story gets noticed.

So read on and discover just how easy it is to gather the essential facts of your story.

CHAPTER 4

The 5Ws: How To Gather The Facts To Include In Your Story

NOW IS NOT the time for complexity. Now is the time for simplicity. For this first stage of the process, you are going to provide five answers to five questions. There will be time to add additional detail and finesse it later. For now, all you need to provide is the higher-level answers to the following five questions: who, what, when, where, why?

So let's have our first example story to help you get a better idea of the length and detail of the answers you will need to provide.

The year is 1825, the place is Washington DC, a portrait painter working away from home receives a letter by horseman that reads: "Your dear wife is convalescent". On hearing the news, the gentleman immediately leaves the capital to be by her side. Covering over 300 miles, stopping only for absolute necessities, he finally arrives in Connecticut, only to find that not only has his wife died but she has already been buried. He is distraught; it had taken, in his mind, far too long for the notification to arrive. Without delay, he sets about inventing a means for rapid, long distance communication so that no one will ever have to suffer the way he has again. That man's name is Samuel Morse, better known as the inventor of Morse code.

So let's use the 5Ws to bring out the facts behind the Morse story.

Who is it about?

Samuel Morse, a portrait painter who became better known as the inventor of Morse code.

What happened?

He was working away from home when he received news that his wife was ill. Due to having to rely on a horse to deliver the news, it meant that by the time he reached her she was already buried. Consequently, Samuel Morse invented a useful rapid communication technique so that no one would ever have to suffer the way he did.

When did it take place?

1825.

Where did it take place?
Between Washington DC and Connecticut.

Why did it happen?
He invented Morse Code because his wife fell ill whilst he was
working away from home and by the time he got to her she had
already been buried.

Everything that Morse did in the story was directly related to
the problem he faced. The problem put into motion a powerful
motive for him to realise his goal. Had he not faced that terrible
series of events then he probably wouldn't have invented Morse
code. So now you must take a moment to consider the problem
the hero of your story faced and the goal they want to achieve.
Whether you chose one of the seven story ideas from the list in
the previous chapter or one of your own, right now you need
to take a moment to understand and note the goal. Getting this
right will provide the essential motivating ingredient that will
ensure the story has a point and keeps moving forward towards
it.

So when you answer the 5Ws questions in a moment you must
include the problems you overcame to achieve that goal. You
must also ensure you include any information that adds context
to the story, e.g. dates and places. For example in the Morse story
the places and the year makes it clear that Morse could not have
jumped on a flight to Connecticut nor sent a text message to
inform loved ones he was on his way.

Now it's time for you to answer the 5Ws. Open up your favourite device to take notes on, or you can use the notes pages at the back of the book.

If you are a deep thinker and feel an urge to provide every detail as you go about answering the questions that follow then please, for your own sanity, just button it. Simple answers to simple questions are all that is required and don't try to come up with a title: you will learn how to do that later.

Who (or what) is your story about?

What happened?

When did it take place?

Where did it take place?

Why did it happen?

In everyday life, you stop for lunch, pick up the kids from school, wait for a train and answer scores of emails. Storytelling demands that we dismiss irrelevant interactions. The parts you must edit out are those that do not add context to the story or move it towards the goal. So work through your answers to the five questions and strike through anything that does not add context, provide a sense of where and when the story took place, explain why an event occurred, or move the story forward towards the goal.

By answering the 5Ws you will have the basic content required to create your story, but this part of the process only furnishes you with the raw facts, not the story itself. Now you must probe those facts to see if they contain any of the stuff that sparks interest, and that's the next step to creating your story: The 4Ps.

CHAPTER 5

The 4Ps: The Stuff That Creates Interest

WHEN A SENIOR news editor first suggested to me that you could boil down the things people are interested in to just four categories, I was suspicious, to say the least. My first thought was that everyone is different and as such they have personal likes and dislikes.

That news editor kindly shared with me these four categories and I have successfully used this method to ensure my clients' work gets noticed.

So the 4Ps that arouse curiosity and cause people to want to know more are Princes, Purses, Pets, and Places. The 4Ps do not need to be the subject of your story but if your story can include one or more of the 4Ps then that's great.

Let's look at each one of these 4Ps in more detail.

Princes: A Prince is anyone or anything you can name, but you don't need to explain. Richard Branson is a Prince: you do not need to mention that he is the founder of Virgin. Google is also a Prince. It's not a person, but things can be Princes too: you can just say Google and you do not need to go into detail about how it provides Web-related services and products. Within your own business, your CEO is a Prince as is the receptionist. A Prince is anyone or thing that you can name to your audience, but you don't need to explain. Is there a Prince in your story? Someone or something that is familiar and your audience will immediately recognise without prompting?

Pets: We love our pets more than our neighbours and in some cases, our own flesh and blood. They star in films, TV, adverts, magazines and they dominate the Web. Their cuddly little faces looking all cute. Owners let them sleep in their beds, feed them food that is equal or better to their own and spend a fortune on them when they fall ill. A vet once told me how a customer re-mortgaged her house to pay for the £15,000 surgery bill for her sick dog. The pooch died one week later, but the owner had no regrets forking out the cash; she said it had been worth every penny to get to spend another week with her companion. So don't underestimate the power of cute animals.

Purses: In the western world we are obsessed with money: complaining about it; dreaming of it; spending it; making it; losing and winning it. The more extreme the value, high or low, the more people want to hear about it. From Carolyn Davidson, who was allegedly paid less than £25 for creating the infamous Nike Swoosh (she was later handed an envelope stuffed with Nike stock as a show of gratitude), to the Malevich geometric abstract art consisting of not much more than brightly coloured shapes on a canvas selling at a Sotheby's auction for £40 million. The world loves a story of an entrepreneur that risks everything and wins it all. Equally they like to hear about the billionaire who bets everything on black only to watch it come up red.

Places: Editors know the value of presenting a local angle to a story; this is because the place you were born, live, work, spend your holidays, are all incredibly relevant to you. Places provide context – you can just say the name of some locations and it will conjure up strong emotive images: An evening in Paris, Christmas in New York or a Caribbean sunset. Equally you can use localised places that are familiar to the audience such as the town your business is located, the boardroom or the local coffee shop. So take a moment to see if a location can be used to add context to your story.

So let's hear another example story that uses one of the 4Ps: this time it's a story that Ian Sanders shared with me whilst we were writing our first book together: 'Zoom! The Faster Way to Make Your Business Idea Happen'. Ian told me about Charlie Bickford who, whilst running a plastering company, got fed up with the bolts he was using as they couldn't get a decent grip on old brickwork. Frustrated with the failing bolts Charlie set about inventing his own better bolts to solve the problem. After much experimentation, Charlie created the Excalibur Screw Bolt that could sit tight in old brickwork. One of Charlie's first jobs was to repair the riding school roof at Buckingham Palace. During a storm a part of the roof had blown down and to repair it required bolts that would hold fast in old brickwork. Charlie's bolts proved to be a great success and since then Charlie has provided his bolts for an impressive range of engineering projects, including the Olympic Stadium in Atlanta and the Gotthard Tunnel in Switzerland. Excalibur is not a global brand with offices in every major city; it's 75-year-old Charlie operating from a nondescript trading estate in Essex. He can't match his large competitors on marketing or advertising spends, but he has his story. When a site manager needs bolts that can hold firm in old brickwork, they may just call the guy that fixed the Queen of England's roof, giving Charlie's story the power to convert into sales.

Charlie could have fixed a hundred roofs and each time his bolt performs perfectly well, but would anyone really care about that? On the other hand, when Charlie fixes the roof of Buckingham Palace it suddenly stops being about roofs and becomes 'fit for a Queen'. So you can see that having a Prince in your story, in the case of Charlie's story the Queen of England, will pique the interest in people and make your story more likely to be remembered and shared.

The 4Ps provide a simple way for you to sanity check your work and ensure you haven't missed out the stuff that, although people seldom admit it, they like to hear about.

So is there a Prince, a Pet, a Purse or a Place that you can include in your story? If there is then go to your notes and add it in now.

The next stage is to organise the content you have so far into the tried and tested three-act structure.

Giving your story structure or plot makes it easier for you to tell and easier for the recipient to understand as we have become used to hearing stories delivered in the three-acts since childhood. If you ignore the structure of the three-acts then your story could easily end up as a set of random occurrences. There's a well-known idiom that describes this, namely, losing the plot.

So get ready to learn the method that will convert your content into your story.

CHAPTER 6

The 3 Acts: How To Organise Your 5Ws Into A Story

THE UNIVERSE IS controlled by a very definite set of laws that exist to create order, yet we can easily cruise through life without noticing them. The same can be said of stories: they too follow a very clear and definite order, yet because we emotionally engage with them we usually fail to notice how they are logically constructed. Once you understand the principles of constructing a story, it becomes easy to create, find, remember and use them for your own ends. Stories contain three distinct parts and follow a very definite sequence, which are commonly known as the 3 Acts.

Act 1: An inciting incident, otherwise known as the problem or obstacle

The objective of Act 1 is to gain the interest of your audience. To do this, you must set out a problem or obstacle and introduce the person who will attempt to overcome it. By introducing a problem or obstacle, you will set in motion a natural desire driven by curiosity to hear the outcome. Now you have the audience's attention you can provide some additional information that will help provide context. So from your 5Ws you can include in Act 1 the Who? Why (that's the inciting incident/problem/obstacle)? When? and Where? Saving the 'What happened?' for Act 2.

Act 2: Conflict or struggle

Stories come to life when there is a conflict or struggle. For example, the bank that refused you a loan starving you of progression, a technological challenge that seemed impossible to solve, or a looming deadline. The conflict or struggle provides the resistance for the hero to push back against thus creating tension, and nothing holds an audience's attention quite like tension. If they were keen to hear what would happen next during act one, now with the added conflict you should have their undivided attention as they fully engage in your story, curious to hear the resolve.

So right now, look at the facts you gathered in the 5Ws – can you see the conflict? If not then go back over the questions and add it in. Don't tell me you don't have any – I have never met anyone in business that hasn't faced challenges; those challenges are what you are looking for.

Act 3: The Resolve

The resolve closes the story after your hero overcomes the struggle that took place in Act 2. It's the moment where the tension ends, preferably via some novel, surprising, dramatic or brave act such as a last chance gamble. Act 3 is where you demonstrate to your audience what the hero of the story, which is probably you, learned as a result of overcoming the struggle. The resolve can also be used to highlight what you stand for, the additional value you can now offer thanks to the unique journey you have experienced, or what the world will look like once you've achieved your vision. So when you are writing Act 3 ask yourself, as a result of the struggle during Act 2, what's different?

Use descriptive words to bring the resolve to life, to draw mental pictures in the mind of the audience so they can visualise this part of the story and see the point you are trying to make.

Let's have another example story to help demonstrate the three acts.

Every year in a remote field in Wales, a group of extraordinary people converge from around the world to live under canvas, swap stories and get inspired. The 2012 'Do Lectures' were blessed with a typical Welsh spring so any shelter made for a welcome break from the constant drizzle. It was under a makeshift canopy that I first met Michael Acton Smith. He may have looked every part the millionaire creator of a children's phenomena, even in a rain-swept field, but as I was about to discover, joy did not arrive until long after he had faced the pain.

Act 1: An inciting incident, otherwise known as the Problem or Obstacle

Michael Acton Smith was born in the early 70s when X-ray specs, Bazooka Joe, and Mousetrap were the must have gadgets and games. In his early 20s, he achieved success with the online gadget and gift retailer, Firebox.com. Firebox was listed as the 13th fastest growing, privately owned business in the UK, but Michael wanted to push his entrepreneurial skills to the limit. He secured a cool £10m backing and spent a chunk of the cash on creating a highly complex and ambitious alternate reality game. The game caught the attention of the press and was even nominated for a BAFTA. But it only attracted a disappointingly small audience. With all the hardware, software and logistics of running the game it wasn't long before much of the cash had been spent. Michael needed a way to create the money his investors expected and he needed it fast.

Act 2: Conflict or struggle

With £10 million in the bank you can afford to experiment, take some risks and see what works, but when that drops to the last million you need to quickly find an idea that will provide your investors with their return. At that point, some people might admit defeat and give the remaining million back to the investors and try to forget about the whole sorry affair, but not Michael.

He knew that the only way to win was to stay in the game and see it through. He told me how one day he started sketching out little monsters on the back of an envelope and in 2007, with the remainder of his investors' cash, he took a last chance gamble and launched an online kids' game, described by the press as Facebook meets Tamagotchi.

Act 3: The Resolve

It was a huge gamble but that last long push to the finish line created the change Michael sought. His ability to keep moving forward, one step at a time, until he finally completed the marathon, proved to be the difference between failure and creating a business valued at more than £150 million. Michael Acton Smith's company is called Moshi Monsters and is loved by more than 75 million kids around the world.

So let's break the story down into even smaller chunks and see what's going on in the 3 Acts.

Act 1: Inciting incident otherwise known as the Problem or Obstacle

We start with some context to get an idea of the era, Michael's passion and his appetite for success. Then we get to the problem in the shape of £9 of the £10 million already spent. You now have your audience's attention and they will be curious to know how Michael resolves this situation.

Act 2: Conflict or Struggle

Michael is in a state of conflict: does he admit defeat and hand back the £1m he has left, or find a new idea and try to make that work? With the pressure on, Michael elects to see the race through and launches a kids' online game.

Act 3: The Resolve

Michael sticks it out. To help make the resolve more visual and memorable we use the analogy of a marathon race: 'he finally completed the marathon' and created a business valued at more than £150 million.

Apart from demonstrating the steely nerves of Michael and his ability to innovate under pressure, the story also teaches us about persistence and can be told to a team who are ready to give up as a way of demonstrating that persistence is often the only difference between short-term failure and long-term success.

By organising your facts into the three acts you ensure it fits with the structure that we have come to expect stories to be delivered in. So take what you've created so far and drop it into the 3 Acts.

In the next chapter, you will discover how to create the all-important emotion that makes stories engaging.

CHAPTER 7

The 2 States: Injecting The Emotional 'Crack' To Get People Hooked On Your Story

---

NEWTON'S THIRD LAW of relativity dictates that every action has its equal and opposite reaction. Stories also demand equal and opposite reactions.

It is an unarguable fact that you can't be in both a positive and a negative state of mind at exactly the same time. The brain can only be in one state at any single moment; it can, however, move at speed between states that are poles apart. Stories are the same: they cannot be happy and sad at exactly the same moment in the story, but they can quickly flip from one emotional state to another. By switching between two states, your story will stir emotions in the audience and keep them engaged.

The good news is that it's not difficult to find those two states. They are simply the opposite of whatever the current state is at any given point in the story: happy switches to sad, success to failure, up becomes down, strong to weak, assurance gives way to fear, laughter turns to tears, hot to cold, fast to slow and what is on is suddenly off.

The story about a rich man that stays rich is not much of a story at all, yet a rich man who loses everything and becomes poor, or a poor man who creates riches, contains the change of state that creates engaging content. Your story can switch states as many times as you see fit, but be sure to allow enough time for your audience to tune into the new state.

Here is another story that will demonstrate how to use those juxtapositions to best effect.

In early 2014 I was giving an after-dinner speech to a group of executives about the power of telling your business story. To help bring my thinking to life I explained that our beliefs drive our purpose in life and when we tell the story of our journey of finding and acting upon our purpose we arrive at a compelling story. At the end of my talk, the event organiser asked me to give a live demonstration of how to find a person's purpose and then turn that into a story. I looked across the room and caught the eye of my victim. I discovered that Steve was the founder of

Ecosurety, a business that helps companies make better use of scarce resources. Now I just needed to find the reason why he started his business in the first place, but Steve didn't seem to know. I took a leap of faith and asked about his family.

Steve told me that his father was a fireman in the early 1970s and was promoted through the ranks to Station Officer. Then, fighting a fire in the late 80s, his father suffered a severe neck injury and was forced to retire, cutting short his career. Steve's father didn't know what to do, but he had always been interested in old cars. With time on his hands, he found enjoyment in rummaging through spare parts at breakers yards and auto jumbles, bringing home rusty bits of old cars and tinkering with them in the garage. However, Steve's mum was less impressed, having to put up with an ever-growing pile of broken parts and wrecked cars in the garden.

Then Steve told the room that one day the garage doors swung open and out rolled a gleaming, majestic, vintage motorcar with his dad behind the wheel. All that discarded junk had been carefully collected, cleaned, organised and crafted back into a beautiful vehicle. His father had found a new purpose. He immediately launched a wedding car hire business with Steve's mother managing the accounts and helping to expand the business into film hire.

When those garage doors were flung open, Steve learned a valuable life lesson that would shape his future. Steve learned that one man's rubbish is another man's gold.

Now Steve helps global companies create value by diverting their waste away from landfill and keeping the material in circulation through recycling. "I hate to see things being wasted, and find myself tirelessly challenging people's limiting beliefs about what's possible. Everything I do revolves around improving our use of resources for the benefit of future generations," said Steve. That is his purpose and his story is the articulation of that purpose.

Not everyone will have a powerful story like Steve's, but the thing is, Steve didn't even know he had a story and he certainly hadn't captured it. In discovering it he found the purpose to his business, and in turn he has been able to use this to help new clients understand why his business exists.

Now let's just bring this back to the two states: by switching your story between states you can ensure it stirs emotions. So let's break Steve's story down:

- Steve's father became a fireman in the early 1970s and was promoted through the ranks to Station Officer. (Positive)

- Then in the late 80s a tragic accident ends his career. (Negative)

- Steve's father took pleasure in rummaging around breakers yards and auto jumbles, bringing home bits of old cars and tinkering with them. (Positive)

- However Steve's mum was less impressed. (Negative)
- Then one day the garage doors swung open and out rolled a gleaming, majestic vintage motorcar with his dad behind the wheel. (Positive)

By flipping between the two states you will move people between emotions and, as a result, make your story more engaging. So, even though the second act, the struggle, suggests that it's all problems (negative), it does leave room for hope (positive) and small successes (positive).

Tease out both the negative and positive aspects of your story and sprinkle them through the second act to provide the much-needed state changes.

So now all that is left to do is to create a headline for your story. When we share stories with people we don't really need a headline to announce it, we just kick off with the story. Online however, we have the opportunity for a subject line, status update or title, all of which can be used to entice people to read your story. The more compelling the headline, the more likely you are to grab attention. So it goes without saying that you need one killer headline.

CHAPTER 8

The 1 Killer Headline: How To Get Your Story Across In A Sentence And Create An Impact

---

HOW MANY BOOKS have you purchased based solely on the title? The story goes that in the 1800s an enterprising printer began buying up job lots of books that hadn't sold very well. He removed the book covers and replaced them with more compelling titles before putting the books back on the market for sale. In doing so, he created a very lucrative business based on an idea that authors' original titles had failed to grab the attention of buyers. How many links have you clicked on based purely on a promising headline? How many talks have you attended because the subject title promised to teach you something valuable? How many videos have you

watched online because the title intrigued you? Now consider
the huge amount of very similar content you must have ignored
because the headline failed to arrest your attention.

To create a great headline, you must first know who your
audience are. Then the role of the headline is to grab the interest
of that audience as fast as possible. That's true if you're writing a
headline for a conference where you want to get bums on seats,
a headline for an internal memo that you actually need the staff
to read, or a headline for a blog.

To grab attention, the headline must go some way to explaining
what the story is about. It's a big ask, but, fortunately, there is a
simple way to arrive at the solution.

It was a beautiful spring morning when I arrived at the very
modern offices of The Guardian. As part of my BBC journalist
training, I was about to meet an old newspaper hack that would
teach me a thing or two about how to write stories. My mentor
for the day wore a Columbo style Mackintosh to keep him dry on
those long door-stopping days, his darting eyes were hard wired
to the part of his brain that constantly asks why and his weather-
beaten face made you feel just sorry enough for him that you
would trust him with details that you should probably keep to
yourself. He was every part the 'hack' and over a foul cup of
instant coffee, served in a stark, white polystyrene cup, he told
me about life on a news desk. He walked me through the process
for delivering the news, focusing briefly on each person's role at

the newspaper. Then he casually dropped into the conversation, almost as throw away, that the editor would often come up with the headline, but it's easy as there are only three types of headline.

When he shared that insight with me I simply didn't believe him. With thousands of headlines created daily, how can there only be three types? The idea sounded preposterous, but then he went on to explain how it works and now my team use the very same technique for grabbing attention on and offline. So get ready to believe that there are only three types of headline and learn what it takes to create one.

1 The Promise Headline

The first type of headline is the 'Promise' headline and it offers the reader a very clear promise.

Example: 'Cure for Baldness Found'

The Promise headline should be uncluttered, shouting very proudly exactly what the promise is and used when your story holds the answer to a specific problem. Don't shy away from including numbers in the headline to make the promise clear. Once you think you have created a promise headline try to remove any words that aren't required. Brevity rules, so seek out the simple articulation of the promise.

Some other examples of the promise headline include:

- 'Create Your Business Story In Just 5 Steps'
- 'The Finance Technique That Will Double £500k In One Month
- 'Lose 10 Pounds In 5 Days'

2 The Intrigue Headline

The second type of headline is the 'Intrigue' headline that will draw people in as they become fascinated to understand the story behind the headline.

Example: 'Man Bites Dog'

The Intrigue headline can be used when your story has an element of curiosity about it. Use very clear language and make it easy for the recipient to understand what the story will be about. Like the promise, keep it simple.

Some other examples of the intrigue headline include:

* 'The Secret For Creating A Business Story Revealed'
* 'What Homer Simpson Taught Me About Business Finance'
* 'Can You Imagine What It Feels Like To Weigh Less?'

3 The News Headline

The third type of headline is the 'News' headline and is defined as: new and interesting.

Example: 'First Humans Land on Mars'

It should be journalistic in its approach, true, clear and packed with urgency. Use it when your story addresses a new invention, approach or idea. Try to imagine your headline on the masthead of a newspaper and ask yourself if you would pay to read the rest of the story. Clarity and volume rule here, so shout out the story with a sense of urgency.

Some other examples of the news headline include:

* 'Why You Need A Business Story And How To Create It'
* 'Silicon Valley's Latest Finance Technique'
* 'New Diet Sheds 10 Pounds In 5 Days'

Remember the 4Ps? Look back over the headlines and see how many you can spot. Now check your headline and see if it naturally lends itself to the inclusion of a Prince, Purse, Pet or Place.

CHAPTER 9

Set Your Story Free

OKAY, NOW YOU'VE learned everything you need to create your first business story. Use the 5Ws to harness the essential facts and then move quickly through the 4Ps; the 3 Acts will help you to organise your facts into the correct order and then apply the 2 States across the second act of the story to give it some emotion. Finally, summarise your story with 1 Killer Headline.

Now you need to start telling your story. Don't hide it away, set your story free, share it, shout it from the rooftops, inspire your audience to share it and spread the word.

To give you inspiration, here are 13 situations where you can use your business story:

1) Face to face sales
These days we seem to have fewer opportunities to actually meet a prospect in person, so every interaction is valuable. Telling a story about your product, service or business is a much more powerful way to connect with a potential customer than ramming the reasons to buy your product down their throat. A story demands attention, then you can frame the client problem, put the client in the starring role of the movie and close with your solution as the resolve. So don't sell, tell!

2) Networking
One of the problems with networking is being remembered after the event and I don't just mean your name, I mean being remembered for what you offer. Sharing your story will make you memorable. Recently a chap accosted me in a car park; it turned out he was the global head of marketing for a large tech company. I had met him briefly at an event, where I had shared a story with him. Here we were nearly two years later and not only could he recall the story, but he knew who I was and what I do.

3) Content
Before a customer buys from you they'll probably search online for content that provides more information about your business

and your offering. In the rush to produce more online content the only way you'll differentiate your work from the competition is by what you say and the way you say it. Present your content as a story and you'll connect at the all-important emotional level and people will be more likely to share it.

4) Pitches

Most pitches are the result of one party (the client) asking other parties (providers) to solve a challenge. So how will the client choose? Price? Solution? Business fit? There probably won't be that much of a difference between the tenderer's price and solution but business fit isn't about widgets and rate cards, it's about you. Take the client problem and using the 5-steps create a solution that demonstrates how you will work with them to solve it.

5) Social

Sharing a story is one of the most social things you can do and the abundance of online channels has made connecting with audiences easier than ever before. Your stories can add meaning to your offering and connect you with your customers via engaging, believable content. There is a growing body of evidence that suggests that the millennial consumer trusts user-generated content over traditional advertising; your business story is a positive shift towards that trend.

6) Marketing and advertising

What interlocks marketing to profits is engagement and one way to achieve engagement is by having a compelling story. When stories are at the heart of the campaign, they engage prospects, get shared and are easily remembered. That means your story, the positive reasons why they should choose you, will live in the minds of potential customers and will be there ready to influence their purchase decision.

7) Internal culture change

The single most difficult change to make in a business is the culture. You can implement away days, set up a task force, even move office, but culture just tends to stick. Stories can illustrate what is expected of staff as the business changes. They can be used to highlight the disruptive nature of bad habits and problems without finger pointing. Equally they can highlight a success in an all-inclusive way. But most importantly, stories can bring to life the values of the company and help everyone understand the vision.

8) Presentations

How many presentations do you sit through each year? How many did you attend last month? How many of them can you recall? Not many if you are attending similar presentations to me. Another unmemorable 60 minutes pass that ends with someone politely requesting a copy of the deck that won't be opened again, unless they plan to pilfer a slide or two from it for their own presentation. Keep your audience engaged and make your next presentation memorable by including a story or three.

9) New business meetings

Each time you present to a prospect you are trying to make a good impression. The question is will the client remember anything you told them after you have left the room? I've had the pleasure of sitting on both sides of the table as a supplier and as a client. As the client, the dullest part for me is when the elected leader tells me about the business. They explain how many staff they have, how they break down into accounts, geography... it drags on. Seldom does anyone tell me WHY the company exists. Which is a shame because I am much more likely to engage with a company that has a reason to be in the room.

10) PR

Most press releases comprise of a pun headline, a list of stats and a quote from someone relatively senior sounding, who is desperate to sell something. Media organisations across the globe glance at these adverts dressed as news and delete them. Press releases still have their place but only if they provide the understaffed news agency with what they need: stories. So use the 5-step process and share a story that will enable the recipient to easily publish your message.

11) Shareholder meetings

As a leader, it makes sense to share information relating to business performance with a high level of clarity. Where the company was this time last quarter, where it is now and where you plan to take it next. Try enhancing the rational financial projections and analytical charts with the story behind the facts. One or two short stories that help stakeholders understand the context of the changing situations in business will go a long way to keeping them on your side.

12) Data storytelling

There are many tools available that can help visualise the zettabytes of data residing on servers around the globe. But the same fundamental problem exists with the presentation of big data as it does with any other factual presentation. You need to make that compelling insight come to life and the best way to achieve that is to use the 3 Acts framework to give your data context.

13) Introductions

You might not think that a Friday night dinner party is the best place to tell your business story, but think again. You never know how some of those new people you've just met might be valuable in the future, who they might know, who they play golf with, where they might work. So as you get to know new people, find an alternative to the 'what do you do?' question – tell them a story!

So don't hold back from sharing your story.

Next Steps

I hope you found this little book useful. If you did then why not share it throughout your organisation and enable everyone to use the power of stories as a way to share information, connect with new prospects, grow the business and create an amazing culture.

Need more copies?
Search Amazon: **Why You Need A Business Story And How To Create It**

Need help finding and telling your story?
David Sloly is available for workshops and speaking engagements.

david@harveydavid.com
+44 (0) 117 214 0011

CHAPTER 10

About the Author

DAVID SLOLY STARTED his career with £70 and a fascination for all things technology. Four years later he sold his small communications business and went travelling. Whilst exploring the world, he became fascinated by stories and on his return studied with the BBC as a trainee journalist where he learnt the art of finding and telling other people's stories. After a brief spell at BBC Greater London Radio, as it was known then, David moved to the UK's first independent production company where he began writing and producing content for MTV, Virgin and the BBC. In 1997, David joined Kiss FM, a small dance music radio station in London and was charged with making the station famous. David used the power of stories to capture the imagination of the youth market. The content went viral, the audience tripled and David won a whole load of awards.

In 2001, David became interested in advertising and, after winning a place on the prestigious D&AD course, he shifted his communications skills to advertising and marketing. He took a role at an international B2B technology marketing agency and worked creatively across global brands including Microsoft, Google, 3M and Dell, again picking up some major industry awards along the way. David was later promoted to creative director and then executive creative director, where he led the agency in the role story plays in brand marketing. As data and technology became more prevalent to marketing, he began to use stories to bring meaning to data and to enhance the customer journey for automated marketing campaigns.

In 2011, David started Infographics Factory, a business that employs story techniques to make complex information easier to understand. Three years later David joined forces with a previous agency colleague, Harvey Steed, and together they established HarveyDavid, a B2B marketing communications agency that provides marketing automation strategy and implementation, content creation, and social media management.

David Sloly
@dsloly

CHAPTER 11

Create Your Story

Use the following pages to create your story.

The 5Ws: How To Gather The Facts To Include In Your Story

First you need to provide answers to the following five questions. You should only include information that adds context to the story such as names, dates, places and any useful information that moves the story forward towards the goal.

Who (or what) is your story about?

....
....
....
....
....
....

What happened?

....
....
....
....

....
....
....
....
....
....
....
....
....
....
....
....

When did it take place?

....
....
....
....

Where did it take place?

....
....
....
....
....
....
....
....

Why did it happen?

....
....
....
....
....
....
....
....
....
....
....
....
....
....
....
....
....
....
....
....
....
....
....
....
....
....
....
....
....
....
....

The 4Ps: The Stuff That Creates Interest

Is there a Prince, a Pet, a Purse or a Place that you can include in
your story? If there is then include it here.

....
....
....
....
....
....
....
....
....
....
....
....
....
....
....
....
....
....

The next stage is to organise the content you have so far into the
tried and tested three-act structure.

The 3 Acts: How To Organise Your 5Ws Into A Story

Organise your facts from your 5W answers as well as any Princes,
Purses, Pets or Places into the three acts.

Act 1:

Who (or what) is your story about?

When did it take place?

Where did it take place?

Why did it happen?

....
....
....
....
....
....
....
....
....
....
....
....
....

Act 2

What happened?

....
....
....
....
....
....
....
....
....
....
....
....
....
....
....
....
....
....
....
....
....
....
....
....

....
....
....
....
....

Act 3

What was learnt as a result of the struggle of Act 2?

....
....
....
....
....
....
....
....
....
....
....
....
....
....
....

Next you need to add that all-important emotion that will make your story engaging.

The 2 States: Injecting The Emotional 'Crack' To Get People
Hooked On Your Story

Now, as you rewrite your story, tease out both the negative and
positive aspects of your story and sprinkle them through the
second act.

Act 1

....
....
....
....
....
....
....
....
....
....
....
....
....
....
....
....
....
....
....
....
....

Act 2

....
....
....
....
....
....
....
....
....
....
....
....
....
....
....
....
....
....
....
....
....
....
....
....
....
....
....
....
....
....

....
....
....
....
....
....
....
....
....
....
....
....
....
....
....
....
....
....
....
....
....
....
....
....
....
....
....
....
....

Act 3

....
....
....
....
....
....
....
....
....
....
....
....
....
....
....
....
....
....
....

Congratulations! You have created your business story. Now go back over the content and smooth out the rough edges so that it flows and is easy to read.

Now all you need to do is add your Killer Headline and set it free.